Street by Stree

OXFORD

ABINGDON, KIDLINGTON, WITNEY

Botley, Drayton, Eynsham, Headington, Kennington, Long Hanborough, Marcham, Wheatley, Woodstock, Yarnton

GAZETTEER SYMBOL KEY

☎ - telephone number

☏ - telephone booking service

@ - email address

🖰 - web address

🖺 - fax number

🖉 - map page number and grid reference

1st edition published July 2008
© Automobile Association Developments Limited 2008

 This product includes map data licensed from
Ordnance Survey® with the permission of the
Controller of Her Majesty's Stationery Office.
© Crown copyright 2008.
All rights reserved. Licence number 100021153.

The copyright in all PAF is owned by Royal Mail Group plc.

Published by AA Publishing (a trading name of Automobile Association
Developments Limited, whose registered office is Fanum House, Basing View,
Basingstoke, Hampshire RG21 4EA. Registered number 1878835).

Cartography produced by the Mapping Services Department
of The Automobile Association. (A03534)

A CIP Catalogue record for this book is available from the British Library.

Design and management for listings section by ey communications Ltd.
(www.eysite.com). Editorial services by Pam Stagg

Listings data provided by Global DataPoint Limited, London

Printed by Oriental Press in Dubai

The Automobile Association would like to thank the
following photographers, companies and picture libraries
for their assistance in the preparation of this book.

Abbreviations for the picture credits are as follows: (t) top; (b)
bottom; (l) left; (r) right; (AA) AA World Travel Library.
Front Cover AA/S & O Mathews;
3 (t) AA/A Lawson: 3 (ct) AA/A Lawson; 3 (cb) AA/C Jones; 3 (b) AA/C Jones

Opposite page
Top: University dons parade towards Oxford's Sheldonian Theatre
Centre top: Christ Church College's Tom Quad
Centre bottom: John Vanbrugh's Grand Bridge at Blenheim Palace
Bottom: The circular domed Radcliffe Camera

Oxford...

of the country's premier university cities, Oxford sits comfortably on the Cherwell and Thames (also known as the Isis). Its colleges, built mainly in Middle Ages from golden Cotswold stone, are usually bustling with students urists. Sightseeing hop-on, hop-off open-top buses and excellent walking are a great way to discover the compact historic city. For shoppers there are r malls, a covered market with small specialist shops and stalls, and endless nd-hand and antiquarian bookshops and modern bookstores to browse. Around rd you will find pleasant countryside and delightful towns including Abingdon e south, and the Cotswolds towns of Witney and Woodstock to the west.

To help you make the most of your leisure time in and around Oxford we have provided a useful gazetteer covering a range of attractions from the historic colleges to museums and art galleries. The nightlife includes cinemas and a variety of venues offering music, dance, plays and comedy. There are lively late-night bars in and around Oxford and quiet, traditional pubs in the surrounding countryside to discover.

Entries are listed alphabetically (ignoring The) under each category heading. The map reference at the end of each entry denotes the map page number in the mapping section and the grid square in which the street/road is to be found, not the individual establishments. We have given the street name, town/city name, post code, telephone and fax numbers and, where possible, email and website details.

TOURIST ATTRACTIONS

Blenheim Palace

Collections at the Palace include paintings by Sir Godfrey Kneller, Sir Joshua Reynolds and John Singer Sargent, while themed tours provide an insight into the life of Sir Winston Churchill and the Ladies of Blenheim. The Palace plays host to musical events ranging from jazz to classical concerts. The Palace Garden features an Italian garden, water terraces, arboretum, rose garden and the secret garden while the park has a lake and the Grand Bridge besides other attractions.

Blenheim Palace, Woodstock, Oxfordshire OX20 1PX
☎ 0870 060 2080, 01993 811091
@ operations@blenheim palace.com
⌂ www.blenheimpalace.com
🖹 01993 810570
✐ Page 4-C5

Christ Church

Founded in 1524, Oxford's largest and most visited college has the biggest quadrangle, and its chapel, Christ Church Cathedral (predating the college), is England's smallest cathedral. The Great Hall has features from the *Alice in Wonderland* stories written by former don Charles Dodgson, better known as Lewis Carroll.

St Aldate's, Oxford, Oxfordshire OX1 1DP
☎ 01865 276150, 01865 276236
@ ralph.williamson@chch. ox.ac.uk
⌂ www.chch.ox.ac.uk
✐ Page 3-F5

English Heritage: North Hinksey Conduit House

Roofed conduit for Oxford's first water mains, constructed during the early 17th century.

Hinksey Lane, Oxford, Oxfordshire OX2 0NA
☎ 01865 772250
⌂ www.english-heritage.

org.uk/server/show/ ConProperty.201
✐ Page 39-G1

Magdalen College

Founded in 1458 by Willian of Waynflete, Bishop of Winchester, Magdalen was among the first of the Oxford colleges to teach science. It is set in large grounds with woodlands and riverside walks. The Great Tower and the Cloisters are the best known buildings.

High Street, Oxford, Oxfordshire OX1 4AU
☎ 01865 276000
⌂ www.magd.ox.ac.uk
🖹 01865 276030
✐ Page 3-H3

The Oxford Story

The Oxford Story narrates the history of Oxford University through a 25-minute indoor dark ride through the past 900 years.

6 Broad Street, Oxford, Oxfordshire OX1 3AJ
☎ 01865 728822
⌂ www.oxford-story.co.uk
✐ Page 2-E3

South Park

The South Park occupies over 50 acres of open space on a slope between Headington Hill and Morrell Avenue. It offers a children's play area and fitness trail besides an array of events for the public.

Cheney Lane, Headington, Oxford, Oxfordshire OX3 7QJ
☎ 0800 052 1455
@ parks@oxford.gov.uk
⌂ www.oxford.gov.uk/leisure/ South-Park.cfm
✐ Page 34-C5

University of Oxford Botanic Garden

The garden has collection of 7,000 different types of plants. Attractions include a glasshouse, walled garden, classic garden, water garden and rock garden.

Rose Lane, Oxford, Oxfordshire OX1 4AZ

☎ 01865 286690
@ postmaster@obg.ox.ac.uk
⌂ www.botanic-garden.ox.ac.uk
🖹 01865 286693
✐ Page 3-G4

MUSEUMS

Abingdon County Hall Museum

Abingdon County Hall Museum is housed in The County Hall in the centre of Abingdon and displays collections unique to Abingdon, England's oldest, continuously inhabited town. The building dates from the 1670s and it is worth viewing for its own sake.

Market Place, Abingdon, Oxfordshire OX14 3HG
☎ 01235 523703
@ abingdon.museum@ abingdon.gov.uk
⌂ www.abingdon.gov.uk
🖹 01235 536814
✐ Page 60-D3

Ashmolean Museum

The Ashmolean Museum of Art and Archaeology is a museum of the University of Oxford. Collections include artefacts and antiquities from medieval era to the present times.

Beaumont Street, Oxford, Oxfordshire OX1 2PH
☎ 01865 278000
⌂ www.ashmolean.org
🖹 01865 278018
✐ Page 2-D2

The Bate Collection of Musical Instruments

The Bate Collection celebrates the history and development of musical instruments of the Western Classical tradition from the medieval period up to the present day. The Collection is made available for study and judicious use by scholars, students, makers, and players, so as to enhance and increase the knowledge of the history of music as well as the enjoyment of historic performance for all.

Faculty of Music, St Aldate's, Oxford, Oxfordshire OX1 1DB

☎ 1865 286261
@ andrew.lamb@music. ox.ac.uk
⌂ www.bate.ox.ac.uk
🖹 1865 276128
✐ Page 2-E5

Christ Church Picture Gallery

Christ Church possesses a collection of Old Master paintings and drawings numbering to 300 paintings and almost 2,000 drawings all. The collection is strong Italian art, from the 14th to 18th centuries and include examples of the art of Sand Pietro, Filippino Lippi, Tinto Veronese, Annibale Carrac Salvator Rosa. However, th are also some fine works b notable northern painters s as Van Dyck, Frans Hals an Hugo van der Goes.

Christ Church College, Orie Square, Oxford, Oxfordshi OX1 4EW
☎ 01865 276172
@ picturegallery@chch. ox.ac.uk
⌂ www.chch.ox.ac.uk
🖹 01865 202429
✐ Page 3-F5

Cogges Manor Farm Museum

This working museum, depicting Oxfordshire rura life in Victorian times, is se an historic manor house a stone farm buildings. Visit can see a farmstead with original buildings and mee the traditional breeds of fa animals. Attractions includ audio tour of the farm buil and displays of farm imple and machinery. There are regular demonstrations of work such as hand milking butter making.

Church Lane, Witney, Oxfordshire OX28 3LA
☎ 01993 772602
@ cogges@oxfordshire.g
⌂ www.cogges.org
🖹 01993 703056
✐ Page 21-G3

Launchbury Museum

ury Scout Campsite, Boars
Oxford, Oxfordshire
5HD

1865 452 457
1865 326 264
1865 326070
age 48-A1

eum of Oxford

museum tells the story of
ity and Oxford University
gh original artefacts,
ge treasures and room
ngs. Admission to the
um is free.

date's, Oxford, Oxfordshire
LDZ

865 252761
useum@oxford.gov.uk
ww.museumofoxford.org.uk
age 2-E4

eum of the History of
nce

resent collection of the
um preserves the material
of past science. As a
rtment of the University
ford, the museum has a
oth in making these relics
able for study by historians
are willing to look beyond
aditional confines of books
nanuscripts as well as
nting them to the visiting
.

Street, Oxford,
dshire OX1 3AZ

865 277280
useum@mhs.ox.ac.uk
vw.mhs.ox.ac.uk
865 277288
ge 2-E3

rd Bus Museum

xford Bus Museum
s origins in the Oxford
reservation Syndicate,
ished in 1967 by a group
husiasts who had the
ght to realise that vehicles
ential significance to
generations should be
before they were lost
time. The museum is
ome to Morris Motors
m, which tells the story
cars and commercial

vehicles were produced at
Cowley.

Station Yard, Long Hanborough,
Witney, Oxfordshire OX8 8LA
☎ 01993 883617
🖰 www.oxfordbusmuseum.
org.uk
🕮 Page 7-E4

Oxford University Museum of Natural History

The Oxford University Museum
of Natural History houses the
university's scientific collections
of zoological, entomological,
geological, palaeontological
and mineralogical specimens,
accumulated in the course of
the last three centuries.

Parks Road, Oxford, Oxfordshire
OX1 3PW
☎ 01865 272950
@ info@oum.ox.ac.uk
🖰 www.oum.ox.ac.uk
🗐 01865 272970
🕮 Page 2-E1

Oxfordshire Museum

The new museum celebrates
Oxfordshire in all its diversity
and features collections of
local history, art, archaeology,
landscape and wildlife as well
as a gallery exploring the
county's innovative industries
from nuclear power to
nanotechnology. Interactive
exhibits offer new learning
experiences for all ages.

Fletchers House, Park Street,
Woodstock, Oxfordshire
OX20 1SN
☎ 01993 811456
@ oxon.museum@oxfordshire.
gov.uk
🖰 www.oxfordshire.gov.
uk/museums
🕮 Page 4-C4

Pendon Museum

The museum houses a collection
of railway relics, and from time
to time special exhibitions are
on display, a recent popular
example being a collection of
Great Western Railway jigsaw
puzzles.

Long Wittenham, Abingdon,
Oxfordshire OX14 4QD

☎ 01865 407365
🖰 www.pendonmuseum.com
🕮 Page 65-G5

Pitt Rivers Museum

The museum displays
archaeological and ethnographic
objects from all parts of the
world. Collections include
Pacific island objects, including
a Tahitian mourner's costume,
collected during Captain Cook's
second voyage in 1773–74;
Hawaiian feather cloaks in
shades of red and yellow; a
wide range of handwoven
textiles and looms; ceremonial
brasses and ivories from the
Kingdom of Benin; a group of
early masks worn by actors in
Japanese Noh dramas; more
masks from Africa, Melanesia
and North America; and
sculpture from all over the
world in wood, pottery, metal
and stone.

South Parks Road, Oxford,
Oxfordshire OX1 3PP
☎ 01865 270927
@ prm@prm.ox.ac.uk
🖰 www.prm.ox.ac.uk
🗐 01865 270943
🕮 Page 2-E1

University of Oxford, Herbaria

The Oxford University Herbaria,
combines comprehensive
research in plant systematics
with a broad range of applied
biodiversity activities.

Department of Plant Sciences,
South Parks Road, Oxford,
Oxfordshire OX1 3RB
☎ 01865 275000
🖰 http://herbaria.plants.
ox.ac.uk
🗐 01865 275074
🕮 Page 3-G1

Witney and District Museum

The museum houses displays
relating to the history of Witney
and the surrounding area
and also has a collections of
archives and photographs. The
art gallery in the museum holds
temporary exhibitions of arts

and crafts, and a reconstruction
of a 1950s kitchen.

Gloucester Court Mews, High
Street, Witney, Oxfordshire
OX8 6LX
☎ 01993 775915
🖰 www.witneymuseum.com
🕮 Page 21-F2

ART GALLERIES AND VISUAL ARTS

ArtWash

ArtWash is an Oxford based
artist-led platform in a working
laundrette. The non-conventional
space of the launderette provides
a site-specific venue for
contemporary arts.

TruWash, 2–4 Windmill
Road, Headington, Oxford,
Oxfordshire OX3 7BU
☎ 0186 574 4075
🖰 www.artwash.co.uk
🕮 Page 35-E3

Four Impressions

Four Impressions exhibits
a selective range of art.
Established in 1995, Four
Impressions has quickly
acquired a reputation as a
gallery dealing in contemporary
art, with a distinctive and
individual style. The gallery
exhibits paintings, sculpture,
ceramics and small edition
prints, including lithography,
etching and silkscreen.

43 Oakthorpe Road,
Summertown, Oxford,
Oxfordshire OX2 7BD
☎ 01865 516556
🖰 www.fourimpressions.com
🕮 Page 26-B5

Modern Art Oxford

Modern Art Oxford is the largest
gallery devoted to modern and
contemporary art in the South
East. Founded in 1965, the gallery
has a national and international
reputation for the quality of its
exhibitions and accompanying
community and education
programme. From landmark
solo presentations to pioneering
group exhibitions, Modern Art
Oxford keeps up to date with the

most exciting developments in international art.

30 Pembroke Street, Oxford, Oxfordshire OX1 1BP
☎ 01865 722733
@ Info@Modernartoxford.org.uk
🖰 www.modernartoxford.org.uk
🖺 01865 722573
🖉 Page 2-E4

OVADA

OVADA (Oxfordshire Visual Arts Development Agency) exists to facilitate and promote access to visual arts for the visitors. OVADA's aim is to develop high quality visual arts and build national and international reputation of Oxfordshire for the visual arts.

21 Gloucester Green, Oxford, Oxfordshire OX1 2AQ
☎ 01865 201782
@ info@ovada.org.uk
🖰 www.ovada.org.uk
🖉 Page 2-D3

Sewell Centre Gallery

Radley College, Abingdon, Oxford Oxfordshire OX14 2HR
☎ 01235 543 000
🖰 www.radley.org.uk/Pages/musarts/gallery/sewell2004.html
🖺 01234 543 106
🖉 Page 56-D3

DANCE AND PERFORMING ARTS

Ark-T Centre

The Ark-T Centre is home to a whole range of ventures including art exhibitions, creative workshops, dance and music. It houses a recording studio for young musicians, rehearsal space for theatre and dance, a performance and concert area and studios for a group of resident artists.

John Bunyan Baptist Church, Crowell Road, Oxford, Oxfordshire OX4 3LN
☎ 01865 773499, 01865 396778
@ mail@ark-t.org
🖰 www.ark-t.org
🖉 Page 42-A5

North Wall Arts Centre

South Parade, Oxford Oxfordshire OX2 7NN
🕾 01865 319450
🖰 www.thenorthwall.com
🖉 Page 26-A5

Oxford Playhouse

Oxford Playhouse has a well-earned reputation as one of Britain's leading theatres. It hosts a rich programme of drama, dance, music, music theatre and children's theatre.

11–12 Beaumont Street, Oxford, Oxfordshire OX1 2LW
☎ 01865 305300
🕾 01865 305305
🖰 www.oxfordplayhouse.com
🖺 01865 305335
🖉 Page 2-D3

LIVE MUSIC VENUES

Carling Academy, Oxford

The Oxford is an independent live music and club venue, offering a range of music styles and established club nights.

190 Cowley Road, Oxford, Oxfordshire OX4 1UE
☎ 01865 420 046
🕾 01865 420 046
🖰 www.oxford-academy.co.uk
🖉 Page 41-F1

Exeter Hall Pub

1 Oxford Road, Cowley, Oxford, Oxfordshire OX4 2EN
☎ 01865 776431
🖰 www.exeterhall.co.uk
🖉 Page 41-H3

The Jericho Tavern

56 Walton Street, Oxford, Oxfordshire OX2 6AE
☎ 01865 311775
🖰 www.thejerichotavern.co.uk
🖉 Page 33-F3

Oxfam House

John Smith Drive, Oxford Business Park South, Oxford, Oxfordshire OX4 2JY
☎ 0870 333 2700
🕾 0870 333 2444
🖰 www.oxfam.org.uk
🖉 Page 42-B5

Oxford Brookes Student Union

Headington Hill Campus, Gipsy Lane, Oxford, Oxfordshire OX3 0BP
☎ 01865 741111, 01865 484715
🖰 www.thesu.com
🖉 Page 34-D4

Pegasus Theatre

The Pegasus Theatre hosts programmes of contemporary performing arts and runs classes on technical theatre, writing and performances.

Magdalen Road, Oxford, Oxfordshire OX4 1RE
☎ 01865 792209
🕾 01865 722851
@ info@pegasustheatre.org.uk
🖰 www.pegasustheatre.org.uk
🖺 01865 204976
🖉 Page 41-F2

The Pit at The Hollybush Inn

35 Corn Street, Witney, Oxfordshire OX8 7DQ
☎ 01993 702438
🖉 Page 21-E3

Rapture Records

The Woolgate Centre, Witney, Oxfordshire OX28 6AP
☎ 01993 700567
@ info@rapture-online.co.uk
🖉 Page 21-F3

Red Lion Hotel

1–3 Corn Street, Witney, Oxfordshire OX28 6DB
☎ 01993 703149
🖉 Page 21-E3

The Regal

Cutting-edge club venue situated in a restored 1930s art-deco cinema.

300 Cowley Road, Cowley, Oxford, Oxfordshire OX4 1US
☎ 01865 241261
@ jason@the-regal.com
🖰 www.the-regal.com
🖉 Page 41-G2

The Wheatsheaf

103 Marlborough Road, High Street, Oxford Oxfordshire OX1 4LX
🖰 www.myspace.com/wheatsheaf_music
🖉 Page 40-C2

The Zodiac

190 Cowley Road, Oxford Oxfordshire OX4 1UE
☎ 01865 420 046
🖰 www.oxford-academy.co
🖉 Page 41-F1

COMEDY CLUBS AND VENUES

Jongleurs, Oxford

The venue has two floors with Bar-Risa downstairs and Jongleurs above. Access can via the bar or directly into the upstairs venue.

3–5 Hythe Bridge Street, Oxford, Oxfordshire OX1 2E
☎ 0870 011 1965
🕾 0870 787 0707
@ enquiries@jongleurs.co
🖰 www.jongleurs.com
🖉 Page 2-C3

CLASSICAL MUSIC VENUES

Holywell Music Room

Holywell Street, Oxford, Oxfordshire OX1 3SD
☎ 01865 305305
@ holywell.music.room@music.ox.ac.uk
🖰 www.coffeeconcerts.co
🖉 Page 3-F2

Jacqueline du Pre Music Building

The Jacqueline du Pre Music Building was opened in September 1995 with a gala concert given by the Medici Quartet and the English Chamber Orchestra in the presence of HRH the Duchess of Kent. Since then it has held events ranging from medieval music to avant garde jazz.

lda's College, Cowley Place,
-d, Oxfordshire OX4 1DY
☏ 865 276821, 01865 276829
@ p@st-hildas.ox.ac.uk
ww.st-hildas.ox.ac.uk/jdp
age 3-H5

Idonian Theatre

d Street, Oxford,
-dshire OX1 3AZ
☏ 8 6527 7299
@ stodian@sheldon.ox.ac.uk
ww.sheldon.ox.ac.uk
☏ 8 6527 7295
age 3-F3

versity Church of St
y the Virgin

ary's, a lively parish and
ersity church, is regularly
as a venue for classical
erts, and occasionally other
s of events.

Street, Oxford, Oxfordshire
4AH
☏ 865 279111
@ iversity.church@ox.ac.uk
ww.university-church.
.ac.uk
age 3-F3

EMAS

on Oxford George
et

ge Street, Oxford,
-dshire OX1 2BL
☏ 712 244007
ww.odeon.co.uk
age 2-D3

on Oxford Magdalen
et

alen Street, Oxford,
-dshire OX1 3AE
☏ 712 244007
ww.odeon.co.uk
ge 2-D3

Phoenix Picturehouse

alton Street, Oxford,
-dshire OX2 6AE
☏ 70 758 3218
@ oenix@picturehouses.
uk
ww.picturehouses.
uk/01865 310594
ge 33-F3

Screen at the Witney Corn
Exchange

Market Square, Witney,
Oxfordshire OX28 6AB
☎ 01865 880645
🖰 www.screenwitney.co.uk
📖 Page 21-F3

Ultimate Picture Palace

Jeune Street, Oxford,
Oxfordshire OX4 1BN
☎ 01865 245288
@ info@ultimatepicturepalace.
co.uk
🖰 www.ultimatepicturepalace.
co.uk
📖 Page 3-K4

Vue Oxford

Ozone Leisure Centre, Grenoble
Road, Oxford, Oxfordshire
OX4 4XP
☎ 08712 240240
@ guestservices@myvue.com
🖰 www.myvue.com
📖 Page 51-F3

OPERA VENUES

Garsington Opera

Garsington Opera, founded by
Leonard Ingrams in 1989, runs
for a month in the summer
and successfully combines a
repertoire of well known operas
with discoveries of little known
works. Garsington Opera has
been keen to promote young
singers and as a result of this
policy, a number of notable
UK debuts have taken place at
Garsington. All operas are sung
in the original language and
there are supertitles.

Garsington Manor, Garsington,
Oxford, Oxfordshire OX44 9DH
☎ 01865 361636
@ office@garsingtonopera.org
🖰 www.garsingtonopera.org
📖 Page 53-E3

THEATRES

Burton Taylor Studio

This small 50-seater studio
theatre is situated at the
top of two flights of stairs,
just around the corner from
Oxford Playhouse. During each

eight-week University term, it
plays host to a wide variety of
student productions, from new
writing or rarely performed
pieces to experimental new
angles on old classics. Out of
term it is host to professional
touring companies or local
small-scale community theatre
groups who stage various
pieces, often newly written,
offering an interesting contrast
to the larger scale shows at
it's parent organisation, Oxford
Playhouse. You are more likely to
see monologues or two-handers
here, rather than an epic musical
with a cast of thousands!

Gloucester Street, Oxford,
Oxfordshire OX1 2BN
☎ 01865 305350, 01865 305300
☏ 01865 305305
🖰 www.burtontaylor.co.uk
📖 Page 2-D3

Creation Theatre Company

North Wall, South Parade,
Summertown, Oxford,
Oxfordshire OX2 7NN
☎ 01865 766266
@ joannacraig@
creationtheatre.co.uk
🖰 www.creationtheatre.co.uk
📖 Page 26-A5

New Theatre, Oxford

There has been a theatre on
the corner of George Street
for almost 170 years. The first
theatre built in 1836 was known
commonly as the Vic and later
as the Theatre Royale, after
the company that played there.
Following a refurbishment in
2003 the theatre, which for a
period of time had been known
as The Apollo, took the name
New Theatre and currently has
a capacity of 1,800. Audiences
at the theatre can see leading
opera and ballet companies,
contemporary dance, hit
musicals and sell-out pop
concerts.

George Street, Oxford,
Oxfordshire OX1 2AG
☎ 0870 606 3500
🖰 www.getlive.co.uk/oxford
📖 Page 2-D3

OFS Studio

40 George Street, Oxford,
Oxfordshire OX1 2AQ
☎ 018 6529 7170
🖰 www.getlive.co.uk/ofs
📖 Page 2-D3

Odeon Oxford George
Street

George Street, Oxford,
Oxfordshire OX1 2BL
☎ 08712 244007
🖰 www.odeon.co.uk
📖 Page 2-D3

Odeon Oxford Magdalen
Street

Magdalen Street, Oxford,
Oxfordshire OX1 3AE
☎ 08712 244007
🖰 www.odeon.co.uk
📖 Page 2-D3

Oxford Playhouse

Oxford Playhouse has a well-
earned reputation as one of
Britain's leading theatres. It
hosts a rich programme of
drama, dance, music, music
theatre and children's theatre.

11–12 Beaumont Street, Oxford,
Oxfordshire OX1 2LW
☎ 01865 305300
☏ 01865 305305
🖰 www.oxfordplayhouse.com
📄 01865 305335
📖 Page 2-D2

Pegasus Theatre

The Pegasus Theatre hosts
programmes of contemporary
performing arts and runs
classes on technical theatre,
writing and performance.

Magdalen Road, Oxford,
Oxfordshire OX4 1RE
☎ 01865 792209
☏ 01865 722851
@ info@pegasustheatre.org.uk
🖰 www.pegasustheatre.org.uk
📄 01865 204976
📖 Page 41-F2

Sheldonian Theatre

Broad Street, Oxford,
Oxfordshire OX1 3AZ
☎ 018 6527 7299
@ custodian@sheldon.ox.ac.uk
🖰 www.sheldon.ox.ac.uk
🗎 018 6527 7295
Page 3-F3

The Theatre at Headington

The Theatre at Headington
opened in October 2002 and
their programme includes
professional productions from
leading touring companies,
concerts, lectures and
workshops.

Headington School, Oxford,
Oxfordshire OX3 7TD
☎ 01865 759138
@ theatre@headington.org
🖰 www.headington.org
Page 34-D4

BARS AND PUBS

Far From the Madding Crowd

A family run, independent free
house specialising in the finest
real ales and pub meals.

10–12 Friars Entry, Oxford,
Oxfordshire OX1 2BY
☎ 01865 240900
@ sophieeld@aol.com
🖰 www.maddingcrowd.co.uk
🗎 01865 792200
Page 2-D3

The Half Moon

18 St Clements, Oxford,
Oxfordshire OX4 1AB
☎ 01865 247808
Page 3-K4

The Living Room, Oxford

Part of the old Oxford Castle
re-development. Designed with
a 'hunting lodge chic' feel.

The Study, 1 Oxford Castle,
Oxford, Oxfordshire OX1 1AY
☎ 01865 260210
@ oxford@thelivingroom.co.uk
🖰 www.thelivingroom.co.uk
🗎 01865 243708
Page 2-D4

The Old Tom

101 St Aldate's, Oxford,
Oxfordshire OX1 1BT
☎ 01865 243034
@ oldtom@btopenworld.com
🖰 www.oxfordshire.gov.uk
Page 2-E6

Oxford Po Na Na

Offering fabulous interior,
inventive music policies, local
bands and popular exotic
cocktails.

13–15 Magdalen Street, Oxford,
Oxfordshire OX1 3AE
☎ 01865 249171
@ oxfordpnn@ponana.com
🖰 www.ponana.com
🗎 01865 203629
Page 2-D3

The Port Mahon

82 St Clements Street, Cowley,
Oxford, Oxfordshire OX4 1AW
☎ 01865 202067
Page 3-J4

Purple Turtle, Oxford

This unique Turtle is housed
within the Oxford Union. It is
situated underground, with
nooks, crannies, alcoves and
a loud dance floor. There are
lots of games including table
football and possibly the lowest
bar prices in Oxford.

Frewin Court, Cornmarket
Street, Oxford, Oxfordshire
OX1 3JB
☎ 01865 247007
@ oxford@purpleturtlebar.com
🖰 www.purpleturtlebar.com
Page 2-E3

Roots Net

27 Park End Street, Hollybush
Row Entrance, Oxford,
Oxfordshire OX1 1HU
☎ 01865 722227
Page 2-B4

The Studio Oxford

35 Westgate Centre, Oxford,
Oxfordshire OX1 1NZ
☎ 01865 245136
🗎 01865 790346
Page 2-D4

NIGHTCLUBS

Bullingdon Arms

162 Cowley Road, Oxford,
Oxfordshire OX4 1UE
☎ 01865 244516
Page 41-F1

The Cellar Bar

Frewin Court, Cornmarket
Street, Oxford, Oxfordshire
OX1 3HZ
☎ 01865 244761,
077 6969 0177
@ info@cellarmusic.co.uk
🖰 www.cellarmusic.co.uk/
Page 2-E3

Lava Ignite Oxford

The Park End Club offers wide
range of music including dance,
cheese, indie, drum and bass.

Cantay House, Park End Street,
Oxford, Oxfordshire OX1 1JD
☎ 01865 250181
@ parkend-oxford@luminar.
co.uk
🖰 www.lavaignite.com/oxford
🗎 01865 790041
Page 2-B4

The Regal

Cutting-edge club venue
situated in a restored 1930s art
deco cinema.

300 Cowley Road, Cowley,
Oxford, Oxfordshire OX4 1US
☎ 01865 241261
@ jason@the-regal.com
🖰 www.the-regal.com
Page 41-G2

SPECIAL EVENTS' VENUES

The Bodleian Library

Broad Street, Oxford
Oxfordshire OX1 3BG
☎ 01865 277180
@ admissions@bodley.ox.ac.uk
🖰 www.bodley.ox.ac.uk
🗎 01865 277105
Page 3-F3

Christ Church

St Aldate's, Oxford Oxfords|
OX1 1DP
☎ 01865 276150, 01865 27|
@ ralph.williamson@chch.|
ox.ac.uk
🖰 www.chch.ox.ac.uk
Page 2-E5

Oxford Town Hall

St Aldate's, Oxford Oxfords|
OX1 1BX
☎ 01865 252195
@ townhall@oxford.gov.uk
🖰 www.oxford.gov.uk/leisu|
town-hall-contact-us.cfm
🗎 01865 252388
Page 2-E4

Science Oxford

Science Oxford encourages|
the study, application and
communication of science,
technology and engineering|
It was founded in 1985 by S|
Martin and Lady Audrey Wo|
SO organises programmes|
a wide range of events and|
activities to engage busines|
schools and the public in
discussion about science.

1–5 London Place, St Cleme|
Street, Oxford Oxfordshire|
OX4 1BD
☎ 01865 728953
@ info@oxtrust.org.uk
🖰 www.oxtrust.org.uk
🗎 01865 791854
Page 3-K4

Tilsley Park

Tilsley Park, Abingdon
OX14 1PU
Page 55-G4

Street by Street

OXFORD

ABINGDON, KIDLINGTON, WITNEY

Botley, Drayton, Eynsham, Headington, Kennington, Long Hanborough, Marcham, Wheatley, Woodstock, Yarnton

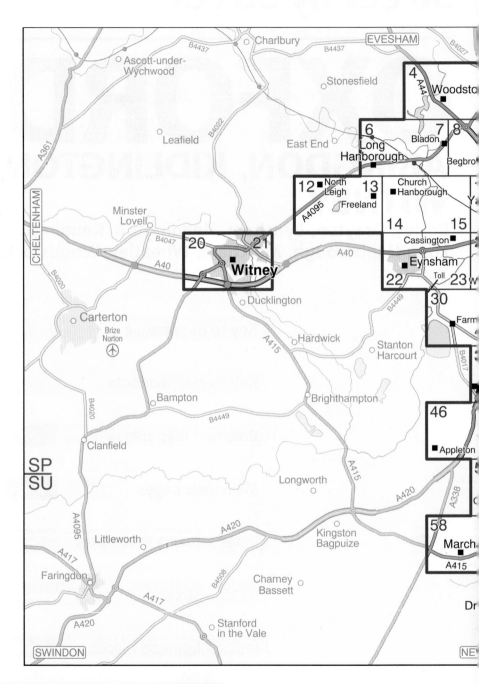

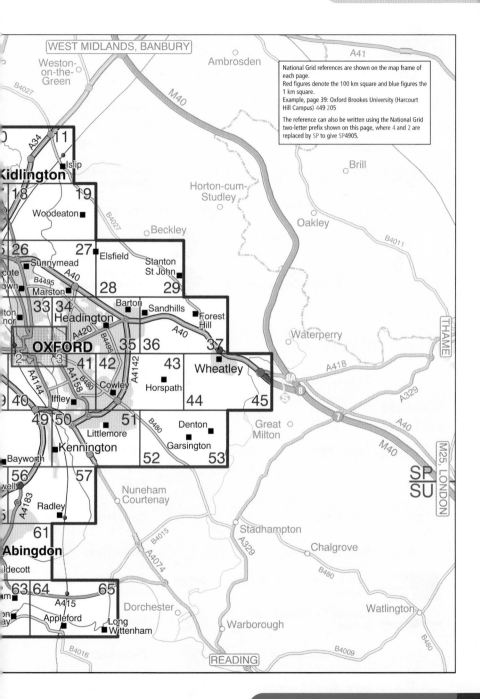

WEST MIDLANDS, BANBURY

Weston-on-the-Green

Ambrosden

A41

M40

B4027

National Grid references are shown on the map frame of each page.
Red figures denote the 100 km square and blue figures the 1 km square.
Example, page 39: Oxford Brookes University (Harcourt Hill Campus) 449 205

The reference can also be written using the National Grid two-letter prefix shown on this page, where 4 and 2 are replaced by SP to give SP4905.

Brill

A34

11

Islip

Kidlington

18   19

Woodeaton

B4027

Horton-cum-Studley

Beckley

Oakley

B4011

THAME

26   27

Elsfield

Sunnymead

A40

B4495

Marston

28   Stanton St John

29

33 34

Headington

Barton   Sandhills

Forest Hill

A40

Waterperry

OXFORD

A420

B4495

35   36

37

A418

A329

41 42

A4142

43

Wheatley

8A

8

A4144

A4158

B480

Cowley

Horspath

44   45

7

A40

M40

M25, LONDON

40

Iffley

49 50   51

B480

Denton

Garsington

Great Milton

SP
SU

Bayworth

56   57

Littlemore

Kennington

52   53

Nuneham Courtenay

well

A4183

Radley

61

B4015

A4074

Stadhampton

A329

Chalgrove

B480

Abingdon

Idecott

63 64   65

A415

Appleford

Dorchester

Long Wittenham

Warborough

Watlington

B480

B4016

READING

B4009

4.2 inches to 1 mile   **Scale of main map pages**   1:15,000

0   1/4   miles   1/2   3/4   1

0   1/4   1/2   kilometres 3/4   1   1 1/4   1 1/2

iv

Junction 9	Motorway & junction
Services	Motorway service area
	Primary road single/dual carriageway
Services	Primary road service area
	A road single/dual carriageway
	B road single/dual carriageway
	Other road single/dual carriageway
	Minor/private road, access may be restricted
← ←	One-way street
	Pedestrian area
	Track or footpath
	Road under construction
	Road tunnel
P	Parking
P+	Park & Ride
	Bus/coach station
	Railway & main railway station
	Railway & minor railway station
⊖	Underground station
⊖	Light railway & station
+++++++++	Preserved private railway

LC	Level crossing
●—●—●—●	Tramway
- - - - - -	Ferry route
....	Airport runway
— · — · — · —	County, administrative boundary
ʸʸʸʸʸʸʸʸʸ	Mounds
17	Page continuation 1:15,000
3	Page continuation to enlarged scale 1:10,000
	River/canal, lake, pier
	Aqueduct, lock, weir
465 ▲ Winter Hill	Peak (with height in metres)
	Beach
	Woodland
	Park
	Cemetery
	Built-up area
	Industrial/business building
	Leisure building
	Retail building
	Other building

City wall		Castle	
A&E	Hospital with 24-hour A&E department		Historic house or building
PO	Post Office	Wakehurst Place NT	National Trust property
	Public library	M	Museum or art gallery
i	Tourist Information Centre		Roman antiquity
i	Seasonal Tourist Information Centre		Ancient site, battlefield or monument
	Petrol station, 24 hour Major suppliers only		Industrial interest
†	Church/chapel		Garden
	Public toilets		Garden Centre Garden Centre Association Member
	Toilet with disabled facilities		Garden Centre Wyevale Garden Centre
PH	Public house AA recommended		Arboretum
	Restaurant AA inspected		Farm or animal centre
Madeira Hotel	Hotel AA inspected		Zoological or wildlife collection
	Theatre or performing arts centre		Bird collection
	Cinema		Nature reserve
	Golf course		Aquarium
▲	Camping AA inspected	V	Visitor or heritage centre
	Caravan site AA inspected		Country park
	Camping & caravan site AA inspected		Cave
	Theme park		Windmill
	Abbey, cathedral or priory		Distillery, brewery or vineyard

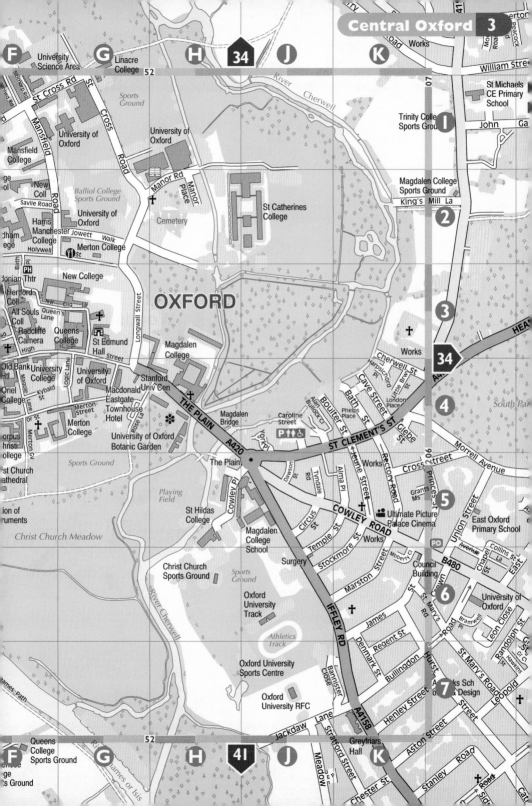

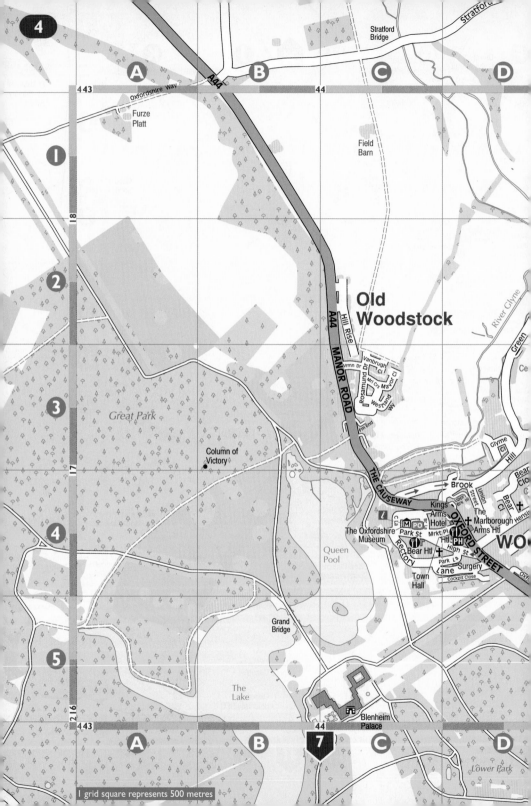

Weaveley
Farms

E   F   G   H

B4027

A4260

B4027

46   47

I

18

Banbury Road

2

BANBURY ROAD

A4095

Shipton Slade
Farm

3

17

Budds
Cl

Banbury Road

Hensington

Hensington
Close

Marlborough
School

Woodstock
Swimming Pool

Woodstock
CE Primary School

Jerinia
Cr

Cls Cl

Plane Tree
Wy

Briar Thicket

Glovers Cl

Flemings Road

The Covert

Hedge
End

WK

Nw wk

ROAD

4

CAMPSFIELD

Upper Campsfield
Farm

Shipton Road

5

216

XFORD

ROAD

A44

UPPER

A4095

E   F   8   G   H

46   47

6

Combe

Stonesfield Rd

Akeman

Chatterpie Lane

A Park Road **B** **C** **D**

441 91 Lane 42

West End

Orchard Ct

Combe Wk

Church Wk

PO

Robin Hill

Combe Gate

Combe CE
Primary School

1

Bolton's Lane

**East
End**

15

2

Combe
Station

River Evenlode

Mill
Wood

3

Millwood
Farm

Millwood
End

Swan Lane

Park Lane

**Long
Hanborough**

Bolsover Cl

Evenlode Dr

Bk Wk
Abelwood
Road

Myrtle
Close

MAIN ROAD

Manor
House

4

Millwood Cl

Slatters Ct

Hurdeswell

WITNEY ROAD

MAIN RD

New
Road

Wastie's
orch

Surgery

PO

Riley Ct

Hanborough
Manor CE School

A40 241

Hurdeswell

BS Cl

Glyme
Way

Marlborough Crs

Isis Cl

Churchill Wy

Roosevelt
Rd

Pinsley Rd

5

Wroslyn Road

Cooks Corner
Farm

Church Road

Pit
We

slyn Road
strial
ate

441 42

A **13** **B** **C** **14** **D**

Freeland

Oakland
Cl

Freeland

arkla

PO

1 grid square represents 500 metres

E

F

4
44

G
Blenheim
Palace

H

I

The Lake

Lower Park

CLOVE ROAD
16

2
The Horse
A4095

River Glyne

Park Lane

Park Cl

Park La

Bladon

PO

Bladon CE
Primary Sch

The Lince

A4095 PARK STREET

Lamb Lane

Church St

Manor Rd

Heath Lane

3

8

4

214

Bladon
Heath

MAIN ROAD

Hanborough
Business Park

Bankside

Lodge Rd

Lower Road

Fenlock Rd

Hanborough
Station

M

Oxford Bus
Museum

Cassington Road

5

Mill Farm

Burleigh Wood

E

F
44

G

15

H
45

8

OXFORD ROAD

A B 5 UPPER C D

445 16 46

A44

Bladon Road

A4095

Orchard Field Lane

The Homestead

GROVE ROAD

Park Lane

2

A4095

Park Cl

Park La

15

WOODSTOCK ROAD

Wolsey Court

A44

Bladon

Campsfield

PO

don CE
nary Sch

PARK STREET

3

Lamb

7

Manor

R

Heath Lane

4

214

Bladon Heath

5

Begbrok

Rowel Brook

Hall Farm

St Michael's Lane

Spring Hill Road

Begbro...

445 46

A 15 B C D

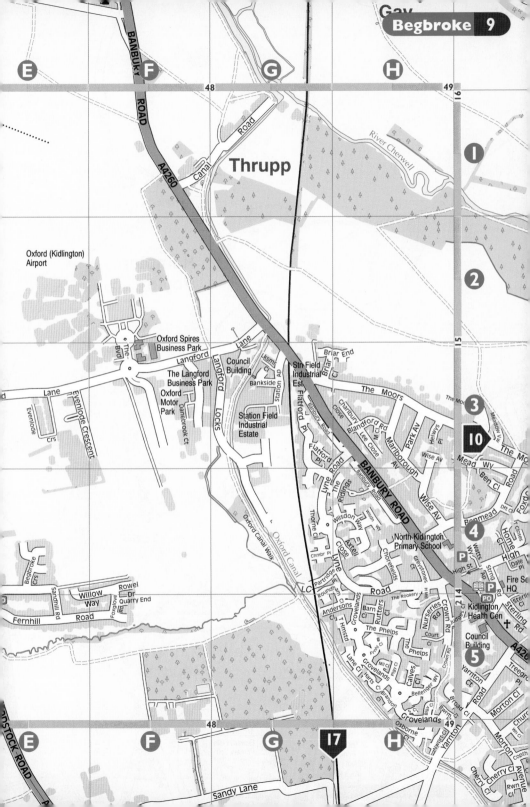

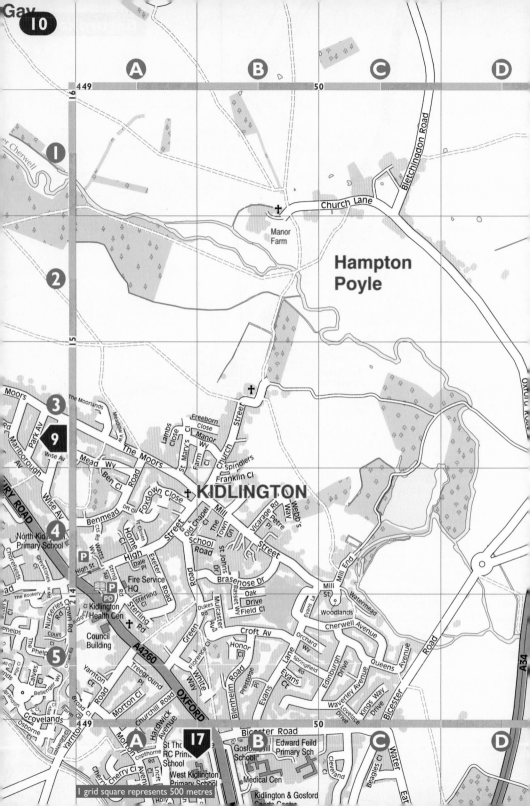

A 4 49 16 **B** 50 **C** **D**

1

2

er Cherwell

Bletchingdon Road

OXFORD ROAD

Church Lane

Manor Farm

Hampton Poyle

3

9

Moors
The Moorlands
Park Av
Wise Av
Marlborough Av
Rd
Meadow Vw
The Moors
Mead Wy
Ben Cl
St Mary's Cl
Lambs Close
Farm Wy
Franklin Cl
Freeborn Close
Manor Wy
Church Street
Spindlers

✝ **KIDLINGTON**

4

North Kidli. Primary School
Chorefields
Greystones Rd
Benmead
Fordown close
ft Closes
Drft Cl
Watts Wy
strng Rd
High St
Dale Pl
Home Cl
Street
Road
High
Road
School
Old Chapel
The
Mill
Street
The Town Grn
Vicarage Rd
Webb's Way
Petre Pl

2 14

P
P
PO
Kidlington Health Cen
Nurseries Rd
Crown Rd
Judges
The Rookery
Exeter Road
Fire Service HQ
Sterling
Sterling Rd
St Johns Dr
Brasenose Dr
Dukes Rd
Mulcaster Av
Basset Wy
Oak Drive
Field Cl
Mill End
Evans La
Mill St
Watermead
Woodlands

5

The Phelps
Court
Calves Cl
Bellenger Wy
Grovelands
Yarnton
Osborne
Council Building
✝
Yarnton Ct
Treeground Road
Morton Cl
Green Way
White Way
Florence cl
Honor Cl
Blenheim Road
Prestidge
Croft Av
Evans Ct
Evans
Springfield Pl
Orchard Wy
Lane
Edinburgh Drive
Cherwell Avenue
Queens Avenue
Kings Way
Waverley Avenue
Lovelace Drive
Bicester Road
A34

A4260 OXFORD Way

A 4 49 **17** **B** 50 **C** Water Eat **D**

Churchill Road
Hardwick Avenue
Copthorne Rd
Cherry Cl
Lnct
St Tho.. RC Prima.. School
West Kidlington Primary School
Bicester Road
Gosfo.. School
Edward Feild Primary Sch
Medical Cen
Cleverand
Beagles Wy
Kidlington & Gosford

E F G H

A34

52 53

16

1

Hampton Gorse

Chipping Farm

2

Field Barn Farm

B4027

15

A34

BLETCHINGDON

3

ROAD

Islip Station

Islip Bletchingdon Road

Conyger Close

Cr Cl

Surgery

Dr Souths CE Prim Sch

Hilltop Gdns

North St

4

Kidlington Road

Church Close

HIGH ST

Middle Middle Street

Lower Street

214

Islip

Church Lane

KING'S HEAD LA

Mill

The Rise

The Wk

The Way

LC

Mill Farm

Lane

Street

Mill

Collice Street

Bridge St

WHEATLEY ROAD

5

E F G 19 H

52 53

Northfield Farm

E F Wroslyn Road
Indu
Estat

Wroslyn Road

Cooks Corner
Farm

G 6 H

41 42

I

Freeland

Oakland
Cl

Freeland
CE Primary School

Parklands

PO

Woodlands

The
Blowings

Church
View

13

Nash La

Hurst La

Beac

Marsh La

Busby
Cl

Walkers Cl

Blenheim Lane

Pigeon

use

2

Broad Marsh
La Close

Websters

Wroslyn Road

Cuckoo Lane

3

14

12

Wroslyn

Road

4

Cuckoo Lane

Bowles
Farm

Little Green
Farm

5

2 11

41 42

E F G H

Barnard Gate

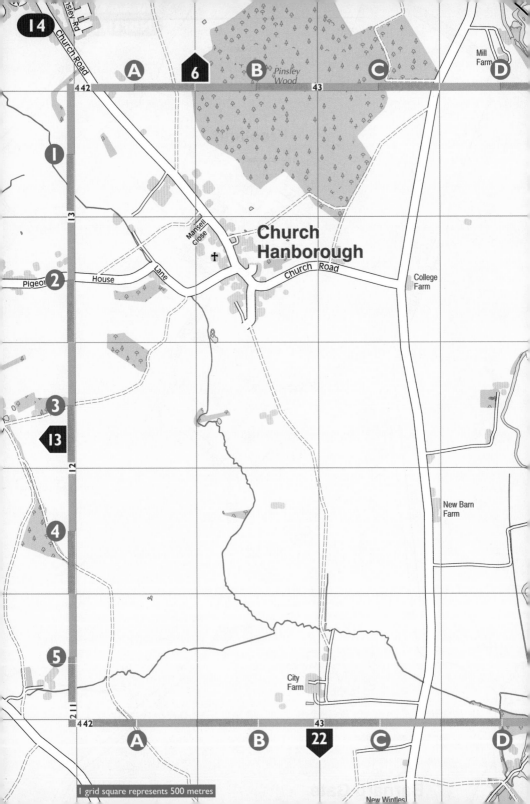

E
Burleigh
Wood

F

G

8

H

45

46

I

13

Burleigh
Farm

Burleigh

Road

2

3

16

12

4

Purwell
Farm

Jericho
Barns

5

2 11

Yarnton Road

45

46

E

F

23

G

Elms
Road

The
Tennis

The Green

Bell
Cl

Old Cl

Bell Lane

Lynton Lane

H

St Peter's

PO

St Peters CE
(A) Primary School

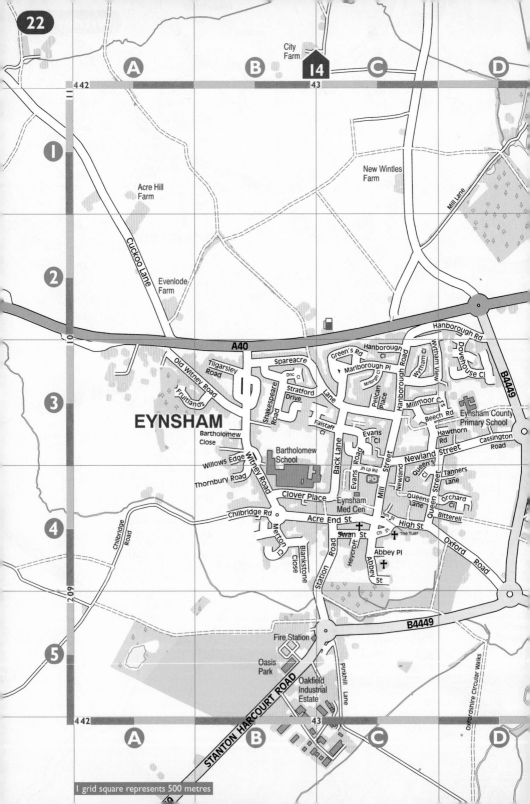

E F **15** G H

45 46

I

Yarnton Road

Elms
Road

The Green

The
Tennis

Bell

Od Cl

PO

Bell Cl

Lynton
Lane

St Peters CE
(A) Primary School

St Peter's

Cassington

Hollow
Furlong

Church Lane

Pound
Lane

Lane Horsemere
Lane

2

Eynsham Road

Manor Cl

Marlborough
Dr

Cassington Rd

10

3

24

4

River Thames or Isis

209

Wytham
Great
Wood

5

OXFORD ROAD

ford Bridge

Thames Path

E F **30** G H

45 46

Swi ford

The Five
Sisters

E **F** **19** **G** **H**

53

I

Woodeaton Wood

Long Wood

Sescut Farm

Elsfiel

2

Home Farm

Cherwell Farm

3

Mill Lane

28

4

Mill Lane

209

Cumberlege Close

Park Way

Lodge Cl

Harlow Wy

Church La

Butts La

Ponds La

Little Acreage

Marston

Elsfield Road

White Hart

Cannons Fld

Southcroft Rd

Barns Hay

Oxford Road

OXSRAD

5

ROAD

B4750

NORTH

54

E **F** **34** **G** **H**

53

Bouits La

Oxford City FC

WAY

St Nicholas Primary Sc

Rimmer Cl

Horseman Cl

Dents Close

Stockleys Rd

Marfield Rd

Borrowmead Rd

Sutton Rd

Foxwell Drive

CHERWELL

Elms Drive

4150 MARSH LANE

New Marston Primary School

Dora Carr

ington Drive

Drive

Meaden Hill

Westlands Drive

John Buchan

Blackwater Wood

Beckley

High St

PH

High Street

Roman W

E

F

G

H

57

58

Sand Lane

New Inn Road

Woodperry Road

Woodperry Road

Beckley Court

New Road

Bungalow Cl

Woodpery Hill

I

Woodperry

2

New Inn Farm

10

Stanton St John

3

snows Lane

Silver Street

B4027

Pound Lane

Church Cl

Mill

Silver Birches

Cox La

Middle Road

4

PO

Hillcraft Rd

PH

Courtfield Road

Middle Rd

PH

209

Shepherds Pit

B4027

5

WHEATLEY ROAD

E

F

G

H

57

58

36

Ashen Copse

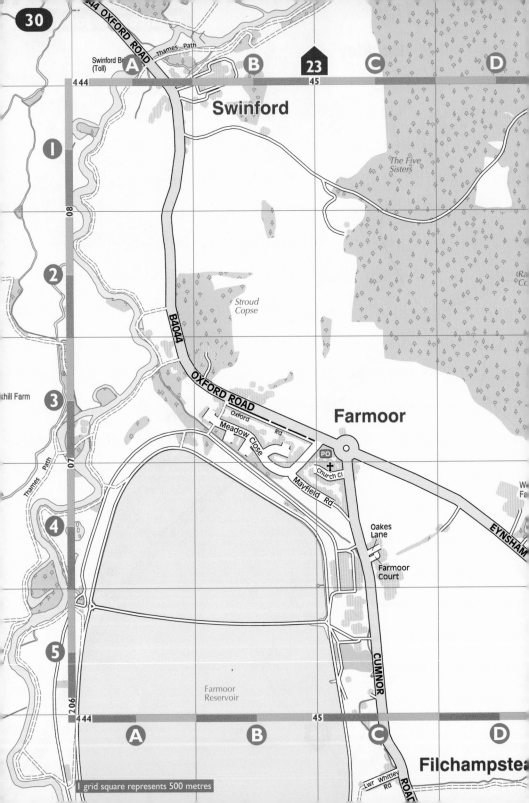

Wytham

E F 24 G H
47 48

I

Wytham
Park

Marley
Wood

2

0¥2
3

32

Oaken
Holt

4
Th..y Farm

Hill End Residential &
Field Study Centre

B4044

Botle

5

B4044
Eynsham
47 48
E F 38 G H
Red Hous.. Red House EYNSHAM R.D
Farm
..dor
..urt
Nobles
Lane
Eynsham
Rd

Dean Court

Third
Acre
Rise

A420

Seacour

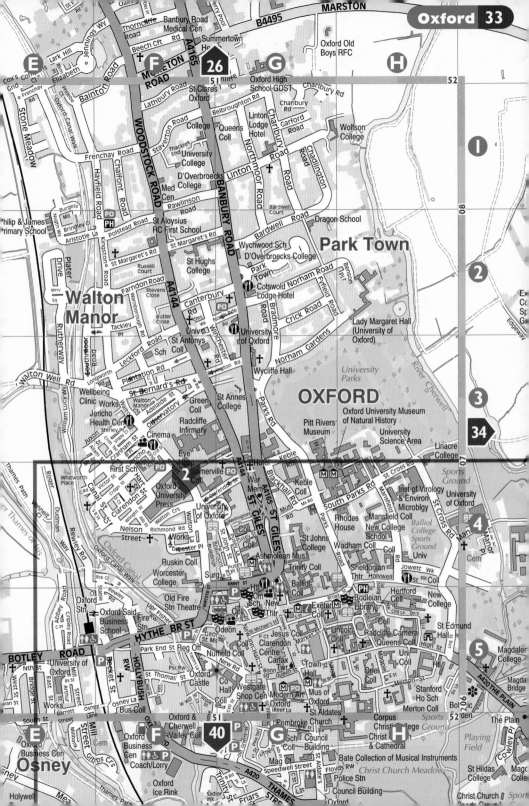

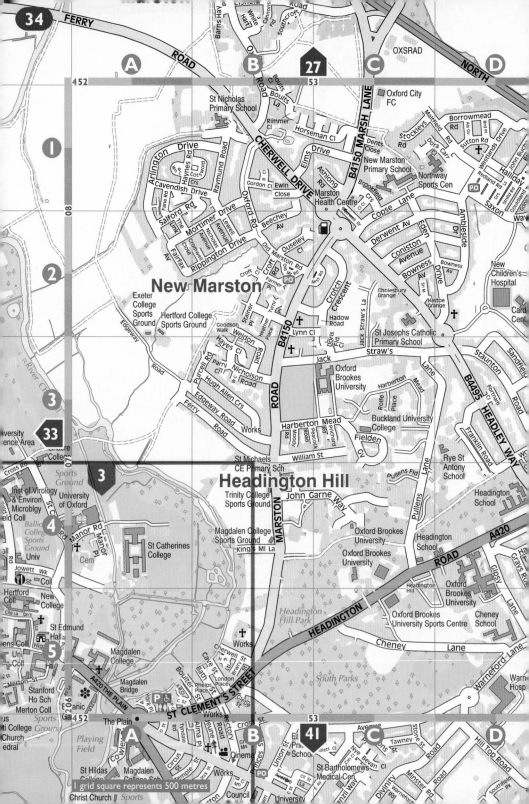

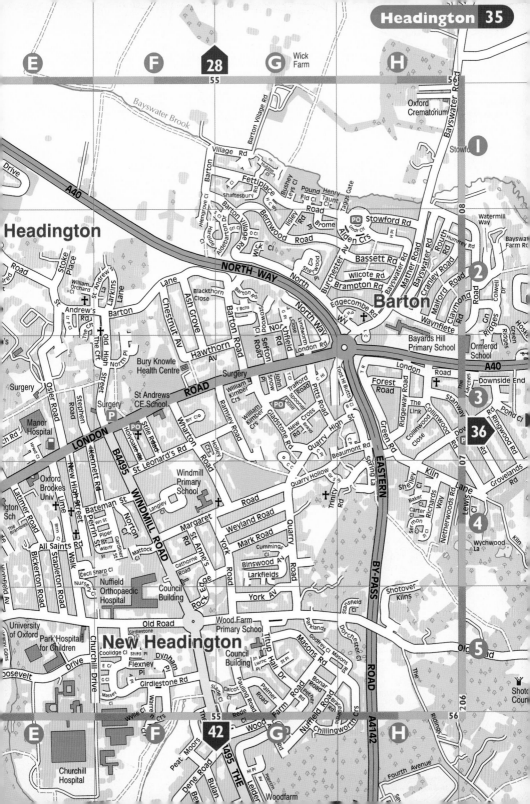

Oxfordshire Way

E   F   G   H

59   60

I

Polecat End Lane

Mickle Way

STANTON RD

Holton Wood

Forest Hill

OX33

ST

Badger Cl

Milton Crs

Powell Close

Manor Farm

Main

Cemetery

WHEATLEY ROAD

Warren Farm

2

08

3

07

4

A40

B4027

LONDON ROAD

Wheatley RFC

Wheatley Park School

The Park Sports Centre

H

5

College Close

206

A40

60

E   F   G   H

59

44

John Watson School

W CE CE School

Ble La

Kiln La

Westfield Rd

Park Hl

Gardiner

Holloway Road

London Rd

Surg

St Mary's Cl

The Glebe

Wheatley Business Cen

Fairfax gate

Littleworth

Littleworth Road

Park

Barlow Cl

High

Therapy Clinic

Church

The Glebe

Church Road

Street

Bell La

PO

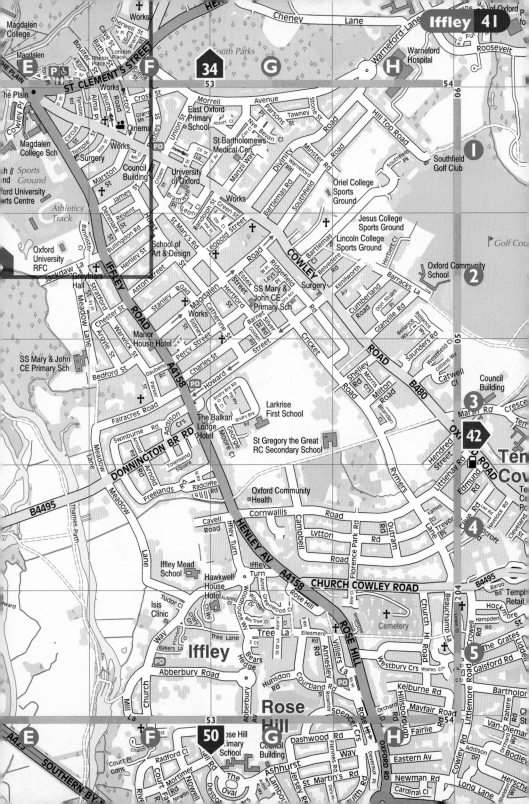

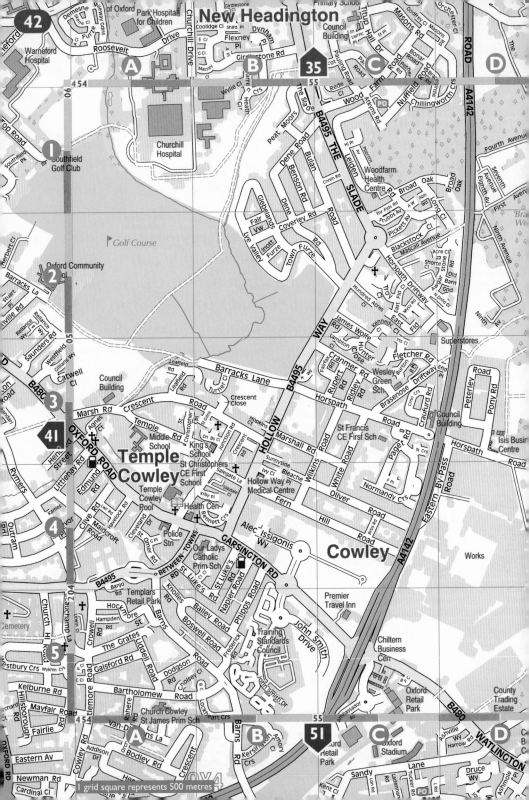

E

P

 over
Country Park

F

36 57

G

H

Old Road

I Littl

Westhill
Farm

Horspath
Common

Open Basenose

Blenheim Road

Blenheim

Gidley Way

Blenheim Wy

Spring La

Horspath CE
Primary School

Collcutt Cl

Fords Rd

Wrightson Cl

Butts Road

Manor Drive

Manor Farm Rd

Church Rd

PO

Gateley

Hill Rise

Centre Rd

Sunny Rd

Valley Rd

Horspath

44

Oxford Marathon
RC

Horspath
Athletics Track

Cuddesdon Rd

Butler

Copcot Cl

Oxford Road

Cuddesdon Rd

3

4

204

5

E

F

52 57

G

H

City
Farm

Northfield
Farm

Oxford R

E F G H

61 62
06

Oxford Brookes
University
(Wheatley Campus)

Holton
Mill

Wheatley
Business
Cen

Old London Road

A40

London Road

Ambrose Rd
Cullum
Leyshon Rd
Miller Rd
The Av
Hillary Wy
Roman Road
Elton Crs
Roman Road

London
Rd

Wheatley
Bridge

Travelodge

I

2

05

Edon
Business Park
Oxford Service A

3

Swofford Lane

River Thame

4

204

5

Cuddesdon Brook

E F G H

61 62

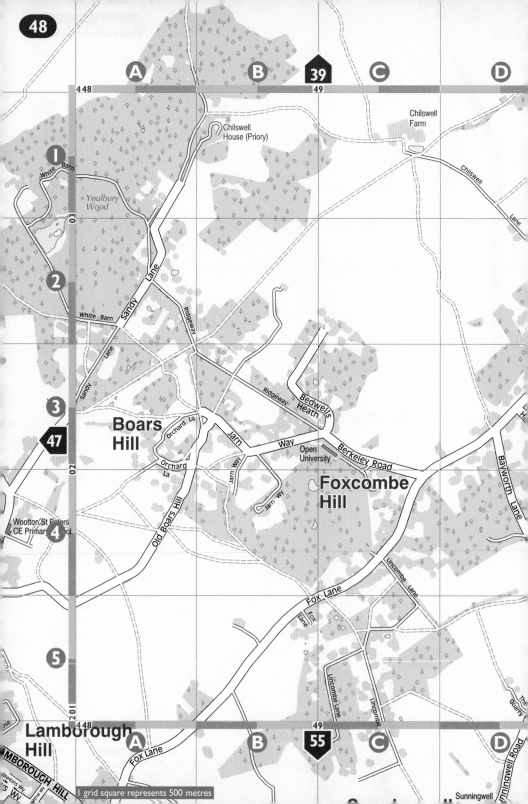

A　　　B　　**39**　　C　　　D

4 48　　　　　49

Chilswell
Farm

1

White Barn

Chilswell
House (Priory)

Chilswell
Lane

*Youlbury
Wood*

03

2

White Barn

Sandy Lane

Sandy Lane

Ridgeway

Ridgeway

Bedwells
Heath

3

47

**Boars
Hill**

Orchard La

Jarn Way

Berkeley Road

Bawforth Lane

02

Orchard
La

Open
University

**Foxcombe
Hill**

Jarn Wy

Jarn Wy

Old Boars Hill

Wootton St Peters
CE Primary School

4

Lincombe Lane

5

Fox Lane

Fox
Lane

Lincombe Lane

Lincombe Lane

The Quarry

201

4 48　　　　　49

**Lamborough
Hill**

A

Fox Lane

B

55

C

D

LAMBOROUGH HILL

Hawkins Wy

Sunningwell

Sunningwell Road

1 grid square represents 500 metres

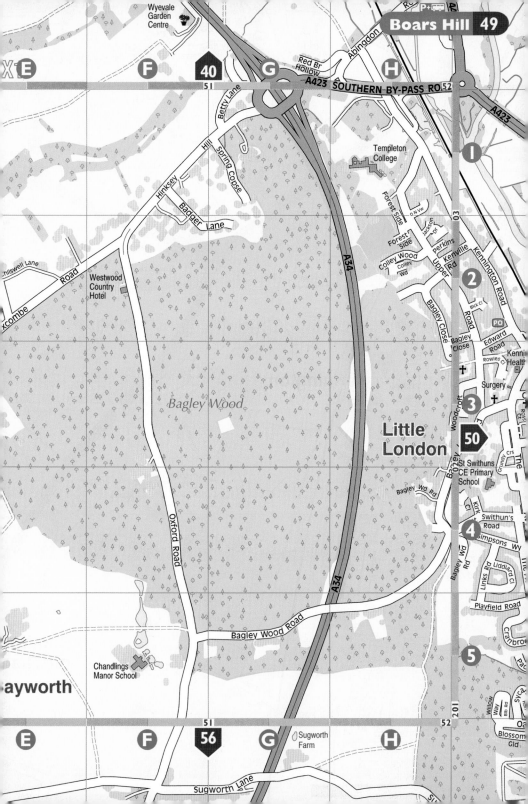

Wyevale Garden Centre

Red Br Hollow

Abingdon

E   F   **40**   G   H

51   A423   SOUTHERN BY-PASS RO 52

A423

Templeton College

I

Betty Lane

Spring Copse

Hinksey Hill

Badger Lane

Forest Side

Forest side

Jackson Dr

ON VW

Perkins

Colley Wood

Colley Wd

Upper Rd

Kenville Rd

Kennington Road

2

Chilswell Lane

Road

xcombe

Westwood Country Hotel

Bagley Close

Bick Cl

PO

Bagley Close

Edward Road

Rowies

Kenni Health

Surgery

Bagley Wood Rd

Bagley Wood

3

Little London

Woodcroft

50

The Crs

St Swithuns CE Primary School

Oxford Road

Bagley Wood Rd

Bagley

Kirk Cl

Swithun's Road

4

Simpsons Wy

Links Rd

Liddiard Cl

A34

Bagley Wood Road

Playfield Road

Cranbro

5

Chandlings Manor School

Grundy Crs

ayworth

Willow Way

Blossom Gld

201

E   F   **56**   G   Sugworth Farm   H

51   52

Sugworth Farm

Sugworth Lane

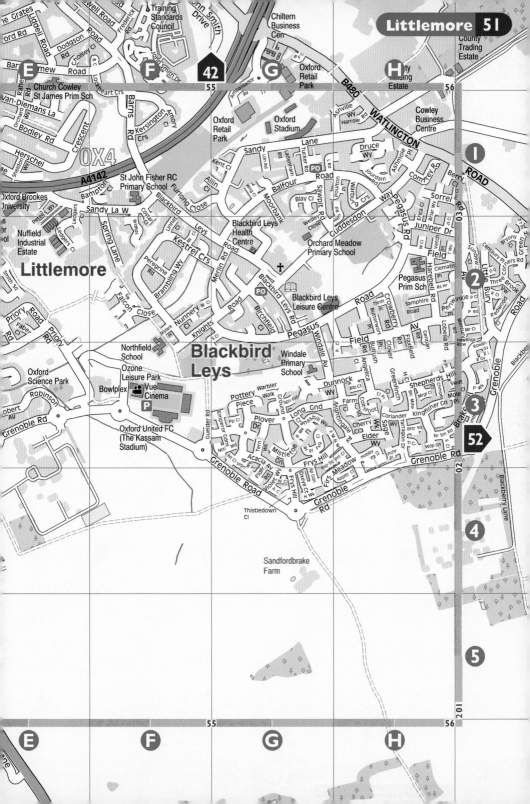

Wheatley Road

Slay
Barn

E   F   **44**   G   H

59   60

City
Farm

Boundary
Business Park

Cuddesdon

†

I

Church
Close

Upperfield
Farm

Field Lane
The Gn

High St
The Lane

PH

†

Wheatley Road

2

nth Manor

Denton
Hill

Garsington
Sports Club

Denton Lane

Denton Lane

Denton

3

02

Garsington

4

Southend

Denton Lane

The Platt

5

Southend

03

201

E   F   G   H

B480

LOWER
RD

59   60

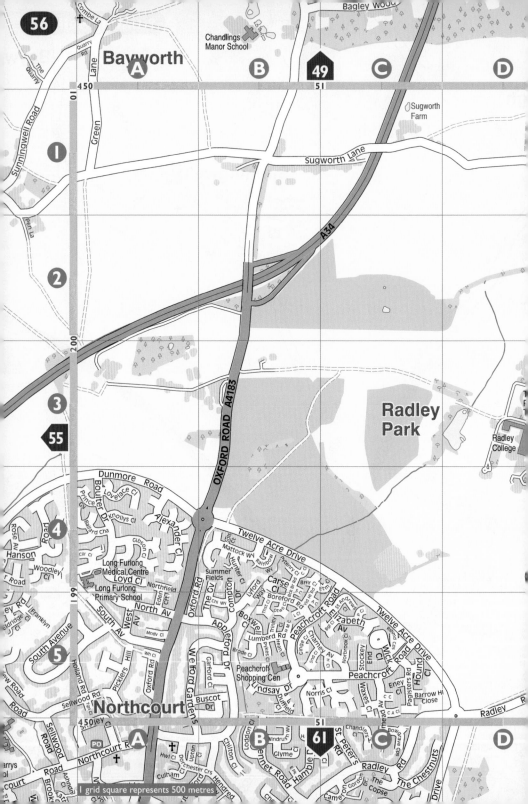

Cranbrook Dr
The
Paddock
Avenue
The Av

Church
Close

Rd

E   **F**   Sandford   Lane   **50**   **G**   **H**

53   54

Willow Way
Hothorn
The
Firtrees
more Crs

Oak Av
Blossoms
Gld

Lower   Farm   Lane

Lower   Farm   Lane

Lower
Farm

1

Road

Kennington

Thames Path

2

200

Park Farm

Thames Path

3

Kennington   Road

Chtnt
Av

Radley CE
Primary School

4

199

Church   Road

PO

Lt Howe Cl

St James
Rd

Ferry
Close

Catharine Cl

New   Road

Sel wyn Crs

St James

**Lower
Radley**

Shaw's
Copse

Radley

oxborough   Road

Turners
Close

Stonhouse
Crs

Badgers
Copse

ooseacre

Radley Station

5

E   **F**   **G**   **H**

53   54

ose
cre Farm

Thames Path

Nuneham
House

E

Gozzard's Ford

F

54

47 Faringdon Road

G

H

48

Hawthorne Av

Close

Sycamore

Cherry Tree Drive

Cherr

Buildings Farm

Faringdon Road

Chestnut Tree Close

Rookery Cl

Elm Tree Walk

Whitehouse Close

Lab

I

Shippon

†

Barrow Rd

2

Sandford Brook

Barrow Road

Nu

3

Blackland

Ab Ho

60

Kimber

Eyston W

Marc Healt

Fairacres Way

A

MARCHAM ROAD

P

A415

Abingdon Four Pillars Hotel

P

4

Superstore

Abingdon Common

5

Norwood

E

Byr

Meadow Farm House

River Ock

E

F

47

G

H

48

62

H

USING THE STREET INDEX

Street names are listed alphabetically. Each street name is followed by its postal town or area locality, the Postcode District, the page number, and the reference to the square in which the name is found.

Standard index entries are shown as follows:

Abberbury Av COW/LTMR OX4 ....**50** C1

Street names and selected addresses not shown on the map due to scale restrictions are shown in the index with an asterisk:

Arthur Garrard Cl OXN/BOT/CM OX2* **33** F3

GENERAL ABBREVIATIONS

ACC	ACCESS	CTYD	COURTYARD	HLS	HILLS	MWY	MOTORWAY	SE	SC
ALY	ALLEY	CUTT	CUTTINGS	HO	HOUSE	N	NORTH	SER	SERV
AP	APPROACH	CV	COVE	HOL	HOLLOW	NE	NORTH EAST	SH	
AR	ARCADE	CYN	CANYON	HOSP	HOSPITAL	NW	NORTH WEST	SHOP	
ASS	ASSOCIATION	DEPT	DEPARTMENT	HRB	HARBOUR	O/P	OVERPASS	SKWY	
AV	AVENUE	DL	DALE	HTH	HEATH	OFF	OFFICE	SMT	
BCH	BEACH	DM	DAM	HTS	HEIGHTS	ORCH	ORCHARD	SOC	
BLDS	BUILDINGS	DR	DRIVE	HVN	HAVEN	OV	OVAL	SP	
BND	BEND	DRO	DROVE	HWY	HIGHWAY	PAL	PALACE	SPR	
BNK	BANK	DRY	DRIVEWAY	IMP	IMPERIAL	PAS	PASSAGE	SQ	
BR	BRIDGE	DWGS	DWELLINGS	IN	INLET	PAV	PAVILION	ST	
BRK	BROOK	E	EAST	IND EST	INDUSTRIAL ESTATE	PDE	PARADE	STN	
BTM	BOTTOM	EMB	EMBANKMENT	INF	INFIRMARY	PH	PUBLIC HOUSE	STR	
BUS	BUSINESS	EMBY	EMBASSY	INFO	INFORMATION	PK	PARK	STRD	
BVD	BOULEVARD	ESP	ESPLANADE	INT	INTERCHANGE	PKWY	PARKWAY	SW	SO
BY	BYPASS	EST	ESTATE	IS	ISLAND	PL	PLACE	TDG	
CATH	CATHEDRAL	EX	EXCHANGE	JCT	JUNCTION	PLN	PLAIN	TER	
CEM	CEMETERY	EXPY	EXPRESSWAY	JTY	JETTY	PLNS	PLAINS	THWY	THR
CEN	CENTRE	EXT	EXTENSION	KG	KING	PLZ	PLAZA	TOLL	
CFT	CROFT	F/O	FLYOVER	KNL	KNOLL	POL	POLICE STATION	TOLL	
CH	CHURCH	FC	FOOTBALL CLUB	L	LAKE	PR	PRINCE	TPK	
CHA	CHASE	FK	FORK	LA	LANE	PREC	PRECINCT	TR	
CHYD	CHURCHYARD	FLD	FIELD	LDG	LODGE	PREP	PREPARATORY	TRL	
CIR	CIRCLE	FLDS	FIELDS	LGT	LIGHT	PRIM	PRIMARY	TWR	
CIRC	CIRCUS	FLS	FALLS	LK	LOCK	PROM	PROMENADE	U/P	U
CL	CLOSE	FM	FARM	LKS	LAKES	PRS	PRINCESS	U	U
CLFS	CLIFFS	FT	FORT	LNDG	LANDING	PRT	PORT	UPR	
CMP	CAMP	FTS	FLATS	LTL	LITTLE	PT	POINT	V	
CNR	CORNER	FWY	FREEWAY	LWR	LOWER	PTH	PATH	VA	
CO	COUNTY	FY	FERRY	MAG	MAGISTRATE	PZ	PIAZZA	VIAD	
COLL	COLLEGE	GA	GATE	MAN	MANSIONS	QD	QUADRANT	VIL	
COM	COMMON	GAL	GALLERY	MD	MEAD	QU	QUEEN	VIS	
COMM	COMMISSION	GDN	GARDEN	MDW	MEADOW	QY	QUAY	VLG	
CON	CONVENT	GDNS	GARDENS	MDW	MEADOWS	R	RIVER	VLS	
COT	COTTAGE	GLD	GLADE	MI	MILL	RBT	ROUNDABOUT	VW	
COTS	COTTAGES	GLN	GLEN	MKT	MARKET	RD	ROAD	W	
CP	CAPE	GN	GREEN	MKTS	MARKETS	RDG	RIDGE	WD	
CPS	COPSE	GND	GROUND	ML	MALL	REP	REPUBLIC	WHF	
CR	CREEK	GRA	GRANGE	MNR	MANOR	RES	RESERVOIR	WK	
CREM	CREMATORIUM	GRG	GARAGE	MS	MEWS	RFC	RUGBY FOOTBALL CLUB	WKS	
CRS	CRESCENT	GT	GREAT	MSN	MISSION	RI	RISE	WLS	
CSWY	CAUSEWAY	GTWY	GATEWAY	MT	MOUNT	RP	RAMP	WY	
CT	COURT	GV	GROVE	MTN	MOUNTAIN	RW	ROW	YD	
CTRL	CENTRAL	HGR	HIGHER	MTS	MOUNTAINS	S	SOUTH	YHA	YOUT
CTS	COURTS	HL	HILL	MUS	MUSEUM	SCH	SCHOOL		

POSTCODE TOWNS AND AREA ABBREVIATIONS

ABGD	Abingdon	KID	Kidlington	OXN/BOT/CM	Oxford North/	RW/EYN	Rural Witney/Eynsham	WITNEY	
COW/LTMR	Cowley/Littlemore	MCHM/KBPZ	Marcham/		Botley/Cumnor	STAD	Stadhampton	WDSTK	W
HEAD	Headington		Kingston Bagpuize	OX/KTN	Oxford/Kennington	WHLY	Wheatley		

A

Abberbury Av	
COW/LTMR OX4	50 C1
Abberbury Rd	
COW/LTMR OX4	41 F5
Abbey Cl ABGD OX14	60 D3
Abbey Pl OX/KTN OX1	2 C5
RW/EYN OX29	22 C4
Abbey Rd OXN/BOT/CM OX2	2 A3
WITNEY OX28	20 C4
Abbey St RW/EYN OX29	22 C4
Abbots Wood (East) HEAD OX3	42 C1
Abbots Wood (West)	
HEAD OX3	42 C1
Abbott Rd ABGD OX14	60 D2
Abelwood Rd RW/EYN OX29	6 A4
Abingdon Br ABGD OX14	60 D4
Abingdon Rd ABGD OX14	62 B3
ABGD OX14	63 H3
OX/KTN OX1	40 D3
OXN/BOT/CM OX2	38 A4
Ablett Cl COW/LTMR OX4	41 G1
Acacia Av COW/LTMR OX4	51 G5
Acland Cl HEAD OX3	35 E5
Acre Cl HEAD OX3	42 C2
Acre End St RW/EYN OX29	22 B4
Acremead Rd WHLY OX33	44 A1
Addison Crs COW/LTMR OX4	41 F3
Addison Dr COW/LTMR OX4	51 E1
Adelaide St	
OXN/BOT/CM OX2	33 F3

Agnes Ct COW/LTMR OX4	42 A3
Alan Bullock Cl COW/LTMR OX4	3 J4
Albert St OXN/BOT/CM OX2	2 B1
Albion Pl OX/KTN OX1	2 D5
Aldebarton Dr HEAD OX3	35 G2
Alden Crs HEAD OX3	35 H2
Aldrich Rd OXN/BOT/CM OX2	26 B3
Aldsworth Ct WITNEY OX28	20 C3
Alec Issigonis Wy	
COW/LTMR OX4	42 B4
Alesworth Gv HEAD OX3	34 D1
Alexander Cl ABGD OX14	56 A4
Alexandra Rd	
OXN/BOT/CM OX2	32 D5
Alfred St OX/KTN OX1	2 E4
Alice Smith Sq	
COW/LTMR OX4	51 E2

Allam St OXN/BOT/CM OX2	33 E3
Allder Cl ABGD OX14	55 H5
Allin Cl COW/LTMR OX4	51 F1
All Saints La MCHM/KBPZ OX13	58 C4
All Saints La ABGD OX14	63 H4
All Saints Rd HEAD OX3	35 E4
Alma Pl COW/LTMR OX4	3 K5
Almond Av KID OX5	17 G1
Alpha Av STAD OX44	52 C5
Ambassador Av	
COW/LTMR OX4	51 G1
Ambleside Dr HEAD OX3	34 D2
Ambrose Ri WHLY OX33	45 E2
Amey Crs MCHM/KBPZ OX13	54 D1
Amory Cl COW/LTMR OX4	51 F1
Amyce Cl ABGD OX14	56 B5
Andersey Wy ABGD OX14	63 E1

Andersons Cl KID OX5	
Andromeda Cl COW/LTMR OX4	
Anemone Cl COW/LTMR OX4	
Angelica Cl COW/LTMR OX4	
Anna Pavlova Cl ABGD OX14	
Anne Greenwood Cl	
COW/LTMR OX4	
Annesley Rd COW/LTMR OX4	
Anson Cl MCHM/KBPZ OX14	
WHLY OX33	
Apley Wy WITNEY OX28	
Appleford Dr ABGD OX14	
Appleford Rd ABGD OX14	
Appletree Cl COW/LTMR OX4	
Apsley Rd OXN/BOT/CM OX2	
Argentan Cl ABGD OX14	
Argyle St COW/LTMR OX4	

Y

Index - featured places

Acknowledgements

address data provided by Education Direct.

tion information supplied by Johnsons

street data provided by © Tele Atlas N.V. Tele Atlas

entre information provided by

entre Association   Britains best garden centres

Garden Centres

ment on the front cover of this atlas is sourced, selected and quoted
ader comment and feedback form received in 2004

AA **Street by Street** QUESTIONNAIRE

Dear Atlas User
Your comments, opinions and recommendations are very important to us.
So please help us to improve our street atlases by taking a few minutes
to complete this simple questionnaire.

You do not need a stamp (unless posted outside the UK). If you do not want to remove this page from your street atlas, then photocopy it or write your answers on a plain sheet of paper.

Send to: Marketing Assistant, AA Publishing, 14th Floor Fanum House,
FREEPOST SCE 4598, Basingstoke RG21 4GY

ABOUT THE ATLAS...

Please state which city / town / county street atlas you bought:

_____

Where did you buy the atlas? (City, Town, County)

_____

For what purpose? (please tick all applicable)

To use in your own local area ☐   **To use on business or at work** ☐

Visiting a strange place ☐   **In the car** ☐   **On foot** ☐

Other (please state)

_____

Have you ever used any street atlases other than AA Street by Street?

Yes ☐   No ☐

If so, which ones?

_____

Is there any aspect of our street atlases that could be improved?
(Please continue on a separate sheet if necessary)

_____
_____
_____
_____
_____

ML093y

continued overleaf

Please list the features you found most useful:

_____
_____
_____
_____

Please list the features you found least useful:

_____
_____
_____
_____

LOCAL KNOWLEDGE...

Local knowledge is invaluable. Whilst every attempt has been made to make the information contained in this atlas as accurate as possible, should you notice any inaccuracies, please detail them below (if necessary, use a blank piece of paper) or e-mail us at _streetbystreet@theAA.com_

_____
_____
_____

ABOUT YOU...

Name (Mr/Mrs/Ms)
Address
                                    Postcode
Daytime tel no
E-mail address

Which age group are you in?

Under 25 ☐   **25-34** ☐   **35-44** ☐   **45-54** ☐   **55-64** ☐   **65+** ☐

Are you an AA member?   **Yes** ☐   **No** ☐

Do you have Internet access?   **Yes** ☐   **No** ☐

Thank you for taking the time to complete this questionnaire. Please send it to us as soon as possible, and remember, you do not need a stamp (unless posted outside the UK).

We may use information we hold about you to write to, telephone or email you about other products and services offered by the AA, we do NOT disclose this information to third parties.

Please tick here if you do not wish to hear about products and services from the AA. ☐

ML093y